RIVERS
OF THE WORLD

THE
AMAZON
RIVER

Karen Bush Gibson

Mitchell Lane
PUBLISHERS

P.O. Box 196
Hockessin, Delaware 19707

RIVERS
OF THE WORLD

The Amazon River
The Nile River
The Ganges River
The Mississippi River
The Rhine River
The Tigris (Euphrates) River
The Yangtze River
The Volga River

PUBLISHER'S NOTE: The facts on which the story in this book is based have been thoroughly researched. Documentation of such research can be found on page 45. While every possible effort has been made to ensure accuracy, the publisher will not assume liability for damages caused by inaccuracies in the data, and makes no warranty on the accuracy of the information contained herein.

Printing   1   2   3   4   5   6   7   8   9

Library of Congress
Cataloging-in-Publication Data
Gibson, Karen Bush.
  The Amazon river / by Karen Gibson.
     p. cm.—(Rivers of the world)
  Includes bibliographical references and index.
  ISBN 978-1-61228-293-0 (library bound)
  1. Amazon River—Juvenile literature. I. Title.
  F2546.G53 2012
  981'.1—dc23
                                          2012009459

eBook ISBN: 9781612283661

                                          PLB

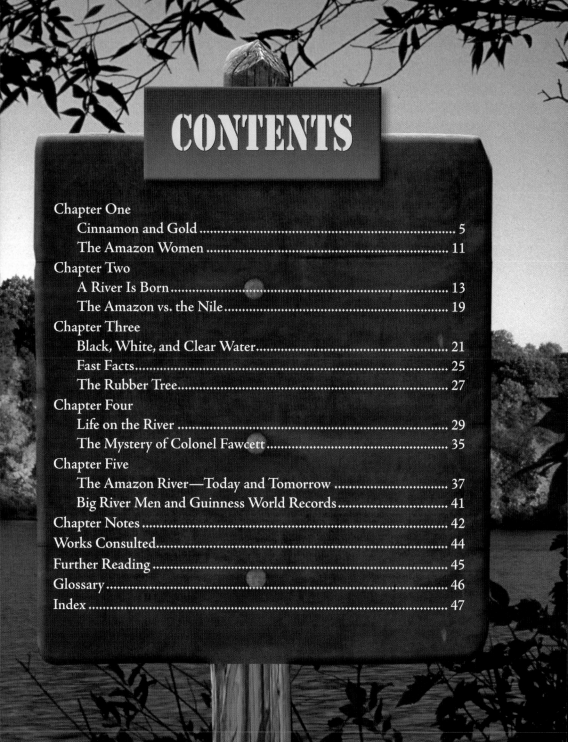

CONTENTS

Chapter One
   Cinnamon and Gold 5
   The Amazon Women 11
Chapter Two
   A River Is Born 13
   The Amazon vs. the Nile 19
Chapter Three
   Black, White, and Clear Water 21
   Fast Facts 25
   The Rubber Tree 27
Chapter Four
   Life on the River 29
   The Mystery of Colonel Fawcett 35
Chapter Five
   The Amazon River—Today and Tomorrow 37
   Big River Men and Guinness World Records 41
Chapter Notes 42
Works Consulted 44
Further Reading 45
Glossary 46
Index 47

Early Spanish explorers searched for cinnamon trees in South America. The highly valued spice was worth a fortune to any country that controlled it.

CHAPTER 1

Cinnamon and Gold

Gonzalo Pizarro may have been sorry he gave his lieutenant, Francisco de Orellana, permission to take some men and look for food. Because it was Orellana who became famous for a discovery.

Both Pizarro and Orellana were conquistadors who came to the New World from Spain early in the sixteenth century. Orellana was a friend of the Pizarro family. The two men had fought under the command of Pizarro's brother, Francisco. Francisco Pizarro was famous as the man who conquered the Incas, a Native American tribe. The Incan empire had been the most powerful in South America.

Gonzalo became governor of the city of Quito (the capital of present-day Ecuador) in 1539. He watched his older brother and other conquistadors discover new places and things. He decided to explore a new region of South America in search of cinnamon.

Cinnamon was a highly prized spice used to preserve foods. In that era, there were no refrigerators.

As the younger half-brother of famed Incan conqueror Francisco Pizarro, Gonzalo Pizarro wanted his own fame. He searched in South America for a city of gold called El Dorado, but never found it.

Food, particularly meat, spoiled quickly. Cinnamon helped disguise the spoilage. Looking a little like olive trees, cinnamon trees had big flowers and pods. The pods were harvested for cinnamon.

Even more, Gonzalo hoped to discover El Dorado, the legendary city of gold. When the Spanish arrived in South America, they heard about a chief from one of the tribes who was supposedly covered in gold dust. Rumors said this tribe also threw gold, silver, and jewels in a lake to keep an underwater god happy.

In March, 1541, Gonzalo set off through the Andes Mountains with 200 Spaniards and several thousand Indians. Gonzalo and his men had no idea what they were in for. The mountains were treacherous. Both Indians and Spanish became sick and died. Other Indians deserted. The expedition had eaten almost all their food and livestock by the time they reached the far side of the mountains.

Flatter land led to many rivers. Rivers meant building boats to get across. It was also the wet season. Frequent rain and lightning accompanied the men. They forgot about cinnamon and gold. Their only thoughts were about food. Forced to kill and eat the dogs and horses, Gonzalo Pizarro and his men were starving.

Gonzalo's second-in-command, Francisco de Orellana, offered to take canoes and look for food. Pizarro gave Orellana his permission along with 55 soldiers, two African slaves, and two friars to make a journey down the Napo River.

Francisco de Orellana was 30 years old. He had lived in the New World for almost half his life, sailing away from Spain when he was 16. He wore an eye patch, the result of losing an eye in an earlier battle.

Orellana and his group left the day after Christmas in 1541. Within two weeks, they found friendly Indians and food, but the strong current of the river made returning to Pizarro impossible. They spent a month resting and recuperating, then continued downstream. They came to an even bigger river on February 12, 1542. Again they met friendly Indians, who told them that further downstream they were likely to be attacked. Orellana had to stop to build a bigger and better boat with help from the Indians they met. Building took time. They had to start with making about 2000 nails. That alone took 20 days.

When they set off in late April, the river took the Spanish explorers on a winding route through thick jungles and more native villages. When food became scarce or the boats needed repairs, the Spanish made their way to shore. They never knew what awaited them. Sometimes they were welcomed by friendly people willing to work for them. Other times, the explorers were greeted with arrows by hostile Indians.

Some of the Indians were naturally hostile to outsiders. Or it could be that word had traveled about the white men. After all, it had been less than 40 years since South American natives had first seen the strange Spanish ship of Vicente Yánez Pinzón along the coast of Brazil. As author Anthony Smith notes, "Pinzón's ships were only several times larger than the dugout canoes of the indigenous people—whom the Spaniards thought to be Indians from India."[1]

Perhaps the most interesting natives Orellana and his men met were a tribe of tall female warriors, who led an attack against them in late June. Orellana called them *Amazonas* after the women warriors of Greek mythology. Eventually these women would give their name to the river. The Amazon River.

The explorers arrived at the Atlantic Ocean on August 26, 1542. Francisco de Orellana became the first European to travel the length of the Amazon River. By then Pizarro and 80 men had found their way back to Quito on their own. Pizarro said Orellana had abandoned him. Briefly, the Spanish government branded Orellana as a criminal, but soon changed its mind. Four years later, he commanded an expedition that tried to travel up the Amazon from the Atlantic. His boat flipped over, drowning him at the age of 35.

It would be almost a hundred years before someone traveled successfully against the current of the Amazon. That someone was a Portuguese explorer, Pedro Teixeira. He began at Belém near the mouth of the Amazon and reached Quito about a year later. His expedition used several dozen large canoes to carry around 2,000 people, including Father Cristobal de Acuña.

Father Acuña wrote about how the Amazon River flooded the forests. He described strange new animals such as the manatee and the electric eel. What seemed to interest the explorers the most was the rumor of gold in the headwaters of the Amazon. But no one ever found the legendary city of gold. While explorers did find cinnamon trees, they were too few in number and too isolated to be a productive crop.

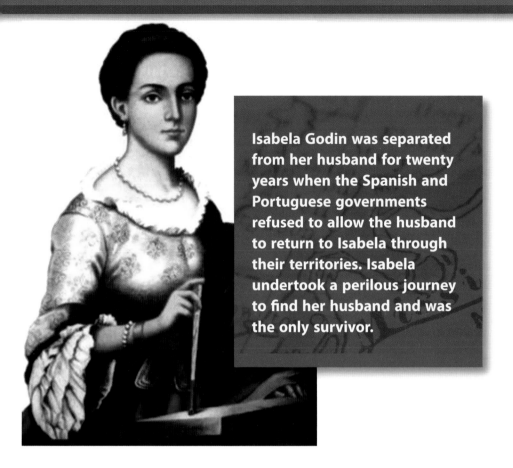

Isabela Godin was separated from her husband for twenty years when the Spanish and Portuguese governments refused to allow the husband to return to Isabela through their territories. Isabela undertook a perilous journey to find her husband and was the only survivor.

Another highlight of Amazon travel and exploration came in 1769, when Isabela Godin became the first woman to travel down the Amazon River. Isabela was a Peruvian noblewoman who married a French scientist, Jean Godin. Godin came to South America as part of a team trying to measure the circumference of the Earth.

When it was time to return to France, Godin traveled down the river to make plans for their voyage. He left Isabela in Quito. She was pregnant with their fourth child and not feeling well enough to travel. However, Godin found himself stuck in French Guiana, a country in northern South America, in 1750. Spanish and Portuguese authorities who controlled the river refused to allow him to return to Quito for his wife.

The Andes mountains

For almost 20 years, the Godins were separated at opposite ends of the river. In 1769, Isabela decided to search for her husband after her last child died of malaria.

The expedition set off across the Andes Mountains. Isabella's two brothers and a nephew traveled with her, along with servants and friends. Isabela wore full skirts and satin slippers like a proper colonial woman of the day. Like Pizarro and Orellana before them, they had a difficult journey. A raft built by Isabela and her brothers broke apart when it hit a log in the Amazon. Their supplies sank to the bottom. They decided to try walking in the forest. Isabela traded in her skirts for a pair of men's pants. Still, the jungle was thick with plants that tore their clothes, and insects that stung over and over again.

One by one, the members of the expedition died, mostly likely of malaria. Isabela refused to give up. After her brothers and nephew died, she "set off again, alone, for eight more days, sustained only by finding a steam of good water, a nest of bird's eggs...and some berries."[2] She finally met with a tribe of friendly Indians who helped her reach the mouth of the Amazon. Isabela was reunited with her husband. They returned to France where she became famous as the first woman to make it down the Amazon River.

There have been many changes since Francisco de Orellana, Pedro Teixeira, and Isabela Godin made their journeys on the Amazon River. But one thing that continues unchanged is the power of the Amazon River. Many people believe that the Amazon River is the mightiest river in the world.

Amazon Women

Amazon warrior

Francisco de Orellana met various native peoples during his voyage down the great river. But perhaps none surprised him more than a tribe of female warriors whom he encountered near the end of his journey. Tall and fair-skinned with long hair braided on top of their heads, these women were armed with bows and arrows.

Even the Indian men who traveled with the Spaniards feared them. Each woman was seen "doing as much fighting as ten Indian men."[3] No men lived in their villages, although the women occasionally captured men when they wanted to get pregnant. Roads connected the villages of stone houses. Reports said that gold and silver were common in the villages. The leader supposedly even ate with gold spoons.

These South American women warriors reminded Orellana of the Greek myths. According to those myths, a race of courageous women knew how to use all the weapons that men customarily used. They were particularly talented with a bow and arrow, spear, and light double ax. These warrior women battled in one-to-one combat against any opponent and often won. Mythology gave these women the name of Amazons, and this is the name that Orellana used for the South American female warriors he met.

The myth of brave women warriors spread to other continents as well. In North America, the best-known Amazon is the comic book heroine, Wonder Woman.

The Amazon River is often a beautiful sight, such as in this photograph of it at sunset. The river can also be very destructive with its force.

CHAPTER 2

A River Is Born

Before the time of dinosaurs, all the continents were joined into one continent, Pangaea. Shifting of the plates in the Earth's crust led to Pangaea breaking apart 245 million years ago.

Geologists, scientists who study the physical history of the Earth, have found a mineral called zircon in the sediment of the Amazon River. Containing isotopes of uranium, zircon works like a clock or a calendar. It tells the age of the area where it is found. The zircon in the Amazon River is believed to have come from a mountain range that once connected the east coast of South America with the west coast of Africa a long time ago.

Evidence from a 2009 study shows that the Amazon is about 11 million years old. Compared to other major rivers of the world, the Amazon is young. The Nile in Africa, for example, is believed to be hundreds of million years old. The Amazon took its present form about 2.4 million years ago. In between, the Amazon was the largest lake and swamp ever

High in the Andes, many rivers like this one lead right into the Amazon.

found on the earth. According to the book *Floods of Fortune: Ecology and Economy Along the Amazon,* "a hint of that vast lake"[1] is evident every year during the wettest season, when river waters penetrate deeply into forests and replenish seasonally isolated lakes.

Scientists have known for a long time that the Nile and the Amazon are the longest rivers in the world. But which is longer? For a long time, it was believed to be the Nile at 4,160 miles (6,695 kilometers). Estimates had put the length of the Amazon at anywhere from 3,903 to 4,650 miles (6,281 kilometers to 7,483 kilometers).

Why can't geographers figure out the exact length? The paths of many rivers, including the Amazon, change according to seasons. Rivers also change their course over time. For a long time, there wasn't an accurate way to measure a river's length.

When the Amazon begins at its headwaters in the Andes Mountains, it is a trickle of water. Other water joins the trickle until it becomes a stream. Melting snow adds to the size of the headwaters as it rushes over and through the Andes Mountains. The stream drains into the Apurímac River. The Apurímac drains into the Ucayali, also known as the upper Amazon. The Ucayali then joins the Maraňon River. At this confluence, the two rivers become the Amazon.

Once clear of the mountains, the land flattens. Here, the Amazon grows significantly—up to six miles (10 kilometers) from one side to the other. More than a thousand tributaries join the Amazon as it flows across the South American continent. Some of these tributaries are 1,000 miles long (1,600 kilometers). It takes the river water one month to travel from its headwaters to the mouth of the river where it empties into the Atlantic Ocean.

The Amazon River moves fast with a current so strong that early explorers were almost powerless against it. The strongest current is at the channel in the middle of the Amazon. This main channel is one to three miles across, but "the Amazon's channel is often several channels. These can flood the land on either side for thousands and thousands of square miles,"[2] according to author Anthony Smith. The channel is also

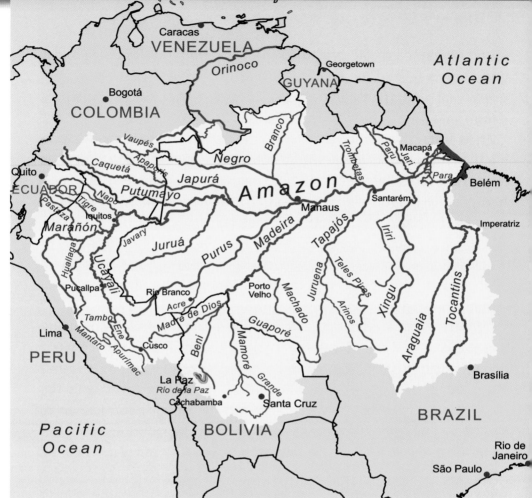

Map of the Amazon River and its main tributaries

the deepest part of the river, five times deeper than the Mississippi River. The Amazon is so deep that large ocean ships can sail up the river through Brazil and into Peru, a distance of 2,250 miles (3,600 kilometers).

Many large river systems have a floodplain or watershed that rivers empty into during periods of high water due to rains or melting snow and ice. None is larger than the Amazon's floodplain. The Amazon River basin measures about 2.6 million square miles. It would cover the entire continental United States, minus California and Texas.

Although most of the Amazon basin receives 60 to 100 inches of rain annually (152 to 254 centimeters), some areas receive more than 200 inches (508 centimeters). The large amount of rain plus snow runoff from the Andes causes the river to rise as much as 42 feet (13 meters). When the Amazon River gets very high, it spills over into this basin on either side of the river.

The Amazon basin is the largest drainage basin in the world. Scientists have recently measured the amount of water or water volume in the basin from space. Doug Alsdorf, associate professor of Earth Science at Ohio State University, states, "Satellite observations are the only reliable options for places like the Amazon."[3]

By studying satellite pictures, scientists have learned that 285 billion metric tons leave the shores of the Amazon River during the rainy season between April and July of each year. This large amount of water creates flooded forests and floating meadows. In fact, it creates a jungle, the Amazon jungle, which is also known as the Amazon rain forest.

Floating meadows in the Amazon

Piranha fish from the basin of the Amazon.

Although 285 billion metric tons seems like a lot of water, this is only five percent of the amount of water that empties into the Atlantic Ocean. The volume and force of the Amazon River is so great that fresh river water extends as far as 125 miles (200 kilometers) into the Atlantic Ocean.

Once the river water enters the ocean, the Southern Equatorial Current pushes against it. The current forces the discharged river water north along the coast of the state of Amapá in Brazil. Amapá's coastline is brackish, a mixture of fresh water and salt water. A large layer of fresh water sits on top of the ocean water.

However, the Atlantic Ocean has a force of its own—tidal bores. These are fast-moving walls of water that flow against the current of a river. They occur in only 30 places in the world. The pororoca, as the tidal bore is known on the Amazon River, is the largest. Twice a year, the pororoca strikes, creating waves so forceful that the ocean pushes the Amazon back for several miles. A crashing sound roars through the mouth of the river as waves 10 to 16 feet high (three to five meters) travel at speeds of up to 20 miles (32 kilometers) per hour.

The Amazon versus the Nile

The Nile River

Look at different geography books and websites and you might read that the Nile is the longest river in the world. That's no longer true, according to the National Geographic Society. The main problem in correctly measuring a river is figuring out where it starts. People once thought that the Amazon started from the Ucayali River, but it actually begins as a stream in the Andes Mountains. Discovering which of the many mountain streams was harder to discover. It was first suggested that the headwaters begin at Carruhasanta Creek on the north side of Nevado Mismi, a mountain north of Peru's second largest city, Arequipa. In 1983, a Polish expedition said it was really Apacheta Creek, which is also in Peru.

During the 1990s, geographers used Global Positioning System (GPS) technology and satellite imagery to measure the river. In 2007, a Brazilian expedition confirmed the beginning of the Amazon River at Apacheta Creek. This information officially placed the river at 4,345 miles (6,993 kilometers) long. This makes it 185 miles (298 kilometers) longer than the Nile River. However, not everyone agrees about the source and the measurements. And with the way rivers change courses, measurements change. For now, however, the Amazon apparently wins the contest of the longest river.

Although the length of these two great rivers is similar, there are significant differences. The Amazon has far more water volume. It flows from west to east while the Nile flows from south to north. Whatever their respective lengths, however, no one can deny that they are two of the world's most amazing rivers.

The creamy coffee color of the
Amazon is due to sediment picked
up from the Andes Mountains.

CHAPTER 3

Black, White, and Clear Water

The Amazon River flows mainly through Peru and Brazil. It briefly touches Colombia. Amazon tributaries can be found in all these countries plus Ecuador, Bolivia, and Venezuela.

The headwaters of the Amazon pick up soil and bits of rock from the Andes Mountains in Peru as it rushes through gorges and over rocks. The water carries this mineral-filled sediment for long distances. The sediment gives the water the color of creamy coffee. People who live near the Amazon River or study it give the name of "white water" to this sediment-filled water. This is different from the white water of the United States, which is the fast-moving, foamy water that moves through rapids.

The main part of the Amazon River is white water. Tributaries like the Napo and Madeira rivers add salts and minerals from old volcanic mountains to the Amazon. The muddy or white water of the Amazon is very nutrient rich. This comes from carrying an estimated 1.2 billion tons of sediment.

White water is one of three kinds of water that make up the Amazon. The others are clear water and black water. "These differences in water chemistry have profound effects on the abundance and distribution of life,"[1] according to *The Smithsonian Atlas of the Amazon.*

Clear water carries little silt or sediment. Most of the clear water tributaries come from south of the main river in an area that geologists call the Brazilian Shield. Some of these tributaries are the Tapajós, Xingu, and the Tocantins-Araguaia rivers. Only one clean water river comes from the north, the Trombetas River.

Perhaps most fascinating of the waters that make up the Amazon is black water. Like the clear water rivers, black rivers carry little sediment. They come from the north. Decomposing vegetation makes tannin, a substance that stains the water a dark tea color. The water is so dark that you can't see your hands when they're in the water. Although dark in color, black water is some of the cleanest water in the world. But the acidic water also stings your eyes if you swim in it. Unlike the main Amazon, mosquitoes are rarely found in rivers like the Rio Negro, an Amazon tributary and the largest black river in the world.

"The confluence of the Rio Negro and Amazon River marks one of the most spectacular meeting of the waters in the world,"[2] notes *The Smithsonian Atlas of the Amazon.* Tourists come from all over the world to see it. Black water is warmer because it absorbs more heat from the sun. This also makes it lighter in weight. After the black water meets the white water, it rides on top of the cooler white water for awhile until the waters eventually mix.

Unlike the thick foliage of the rain forest, there are shorter and fewer plants around the clear and black rivers. That's because these rivers have less nutrients to help plants grow.

The location of the Amazon River is very close to the equator and therefore closest to the sun. The heat, the rainy season, and the Amazon River drainage combine to create the largest rain forest in the world— the Amazon rain forest.

The Amazon is made up of different types of river water. Where the white water and black water meet, it is a known as a confluence. However, it is more commonly known as the "meeting of the waters."

The Amazon rain forest is shrinking, mainly due to deforestation.

The rain forest is so important that when people use the word Amazon, they aren't always referring to the river. Sometimes "Amazon" refers to the rain forest or the basin. The rain forest is one of the chief sources of oxygen for the Earth. As global warming and environmental uncertainty grow, the shrinking of the world's largest rain forest becomes more important.

Often, the forest floor can't be seen due to the large number of plants that cover it. The trees and plants also make a ceiling or canopy overhead. "Perhaps half of all life on earth exists in the canopy of the rain forests," notes author Richard L. Lutz.[3] Occasionally, sunlight bursts through parts of the canopy, but for the most part, the forest stays shaded.

From three to seven months a year, the Amazon rises over its banks to create flooded forests. The river deposits the sediment from the mountains before it returns to the main channel of the river. Sandy beaches and sandbars that appear along the river during the dry season are made from sediment that traveled from the Andes Mountains.

FAST FACTS

Name origin: Named after legendary Greek female warriors called "Amazons" by Spanish explorer Francisco de Orellana

Countries: Brazil, Peru, and Colombia; tributaries run through these countries plus Bolivia, Venezuela, and Ecuador

Major Cities: Belém, Santarém, Manaus, Iquito

Primary source: Stream from Nevado Mismi, a peak in the Andes Mountains

Secondary sources: Over 1100 tributaries; Madeira River and Rio Negro are the longest

Elevations: Average 300 feet (91 meters) above sea level

Coordinates: Latitude of -0.17 (0° -11' 60 S) and a longitude of -49 (49° 0' 0 W)

Mouth: Northeastern Brazil at the Atlantic Ocean

Length: 4,345 miles (6,993 kilometers)

Width: Up to 6 miles (10 kilometers); during the high-water season, the width may be up to 30 miles (48 kilometers. The mouth may be up to 300 miles (480 kilometers) wide

Depth: up to 300 feet (91 meters); average 150 feet (46 meters)

No one knows exactly how many plants have benefitted from the river drainage in the forests of the Amazon basin, but 25,000 species has been suggested. The flooded basin grows a large amount of phytoplankton, which are microscopic plant organisms. The Amazon has the most diverse ecosystem on Earth in part because of the abundance of food available when the forests are flooded by the Amazon River.

Floating meadows also appear in the basin during flooding. Once the water level gets over 16 feet, many of the meadows become uprooted and begin floating. With them are flowering plants like water hyacinths and giant water lilies.

Medicine, foods, and everyday products come from the Amazon rain forest. Over a hundred of the world's prescription drugs are created from plants that grow in the rain forest. Scientists continue to perform tests on the benefits of rain forest plants in medicines. The rubber tree changed Amazonian society in many ways. It led to the development of Manaus, the largest city along the Amazon River.

Tropical fruits that grow in the Amazon rain forest include bananas, dates, oranges, lemons, pineapples, mangos, coconuts, and grapefruit. Coffee, jute, and sugar are important crops from the rain forest. Another very delicious food comes from the Amazon as well. The next time you enjoy a piece of chocolate, remember that it comes from a leafy Amazon plant called cacao.

Did you know?

The Amazon rain forest supplies 20% of the world's oxygen and 20% of the fresh water discharged into the ocean. If the Amazon rain forest disappears, everyone on earth dies.

Rubber Trees

Giant rubber tree

The first Portuguese visiting the Amazon region noticed native children bouncing small objects off the ground and catching them. Upon further investigation, the visitors saw a substance they had never seen before. It was latex from the rubber trees in the Amazon basin. And it was good for a lot more than bouncing balls.

Rubber became a chief industry in the Amazon between 1850 and 1912. Items such as rubber shoes, boots, and knapsacks became popular items. B.F. Goodrich invested in the rubber industry after finding out that rubber was perfect for making tires. It led to enormous growth for the town of Manaus. People getting rich from the rubber industry made Manaus a city rivaling those in Europe.

Hundreds of thousands of men were hired as rubber tappers. Getting rubber from rubber trees is similar to getting maple syrup from maple trees. A tapper makes a cut in the tree and removes a thin layer of bark. Rubber tapping is typically done at night so the sap or latex doesn't dry out in the sun.

In nature, rubber trees are spread out with only a few trees per acre. Europeans felt that moving from tree to tree took too much time. The British smuggled rubber tree seeds out of South America in the late nineteenth century to grow on plantations in Asia. Soon Asia was supplying more rubber for less money. This situation affected the South American market, and prices fell drastically. They rebounded during World War II when the Japanese took over Asian rubber markets, but fell again when the war ended.

Kayapo people of the Xingu
river area of the Amazon

CHAPTER 4

Life on the River

Archaeological discoveries confirm that people have lived in the Amazon region since the end of the last Ice Age, more than 11,000 years ago, and possibly longer. The first humans to live in South America are believed to have come from Asia. Although different cultures existed, it appears that the people who lived in the Amazon rain forest and the people who lived in the Andes Mountain had contact.

By the time the Spanish came to South America, millions of people lived quite well in the Amazon rain forest, which provided everything they needed. They were hunter-gatherers. They fished from the Amazon. Some tribes used bows and arrows for fishing. Others dropped a substance in the water that temporarily stunned fish so that they floated on top. Amazonians hunted game with bows and arrows and blow guns with poison-tipped darts.

The native or indigenous people gathered food from the forest. During the dry season, they farmed.

Their chief crop was maize, or corn. They later grew manioc or cassava, a starch used to make tapioca.

Over 90 percent of the indigenous people were wiped out by the Spanish and other Europeans. The primary cause of death was diseases like smallpox which were introduced by Europeans. In 1842, a Portuguese missionary and advocate of the South American Indians estimated that more than two million Indians in the Amazon area died between 1615 and 1652.

Europeans and American explorers had difficulty with the Amazon environment. Insects were thick in the jungle, and many of them bit or stung humans. Mosquito bites often led to malaria. Other insect bites led to infections that spread at alarming rates. Either ailment could lead to death.

While the native population found the forest filled with many things to eat, the unprepared white explorers starved to death. Some explorers were killed by indigenous tribes; others just disappeared. One of the greatest mysteries of South American exploration is Colonel Percy Fawcett, who disappeared in the Amazon in 1925 with his son and the son's friend.

Humans aren't the only life in the Amazon. "Fish, birds, mammals, and countless numbers of invertebrates meet in these far-flung habitats and remind us that the rain forest and rivers are indeed tightly connected in the evolution of Amazonian life,"[1] according to *The Smithsonian Atlas of the Amazon.*

"The river is the home of over 2400 species of fish, more than occupy the entire Atlantic Ocean,"[2] says author Richard L. Lutz. These range from giant catfish to small, colorful tropical fish often seen in aquariums. Some scientists believe there could be thousands more. Some fish are fruit eaters, such as catfish that eat the fruit of the jauari palm. The tambaqui, the main fish along the middle Amazon that weighs an average of 33 pounds (15 kilograms), travels into the flooded forests, eating fruit that drops from trees.

One of the largest freshwater fish in the world, the Amazon's pirarucu can leap out of water and snap birds out of trees.

The eight-foot-long pararucu is one of the largest freshwater fish in the world. It weighs as much as two men and has a toothed tongue to help with hunting food. Pararucu actually have a lung-type organ that they use to breathe oxygen once every 10 to 15 minutes.

Other species of fish eat meat. One is the piranha, a fish with sharp teeth and an even more ferocious reputation as a "man-eating" fish. Most of the year, piranha feast on seeds, other fish, and the occasional wounded animal. The main danger from these fish comes during the dry season when food becomes more scarce. Piranha may then travel together in large schools to look for food.

More dangerous are the sting-rays that remain camouflaged in the water. They can cause immense pain and even death with their poisonous barb tails.

More than 400 species of amphibians live in the Amazon region. These include 44 species of harlequin frogs, which come in all kinds of colors. Although they are actually small toads, the harlequin is poisonous like the poison dart frog, an Amazon neighbor. Indians often used the poisonous venom from frogs on arrows or darts. Frogs and

toads can be quite vocal and make themselves heard at dawn and dusk.

Nearly 200 species of snakes live in the Amazon region. Almost half are only found here. Many snakes live in the canopy high in the forest, but others are found in the river or along the riverbank. Although pit vipers, coral snakes, and other venomous snakes are among the most dangerous on Earth, the anaconda gets the most attention. This giant snake, up to 30 feet long and as big around as a man, is a scary sight, but it poses little danger to humans.

Another common Amazon reptile is the caiman, a relative of the crocodile. The black caiman, one of the largest reptiles in the world at over 15 feet long, is endangered.

Even more unlucky are the river turtles, particularly the giant Amazon river turtle, which can be three feet long. Turtle meat and eggs were a highly desired food for both indigenous people and early European travelers. Turtle eggs were also harvested for oil. In the early 1700s, 24 million turtle eggs were harvested annually. By 1850, that

The Giant Amazon River Turtle is known to search for the best spot for a nest. Nesting sites are sandy bars in the channels near elevated beaches.

number had doubled. Today, the Amazon river turtle is no longer found in the main river.

The giant Amazon river turtle lays its eggs during the dry season. In the cover of the night, the female digs a hole three feet deep and lays up to 180 eggs. Yet only one in a thousand newborn turtles survives to adulthood following their birth 45 days later.

People can hear birds long before they see them. Shrieks, cries, chirps, and songs accompany travelers as they sail down the Amazon River. Macaws, parrots, parakeets, and toucans are among the approximately 1,300 species that make their home in the Amazon rain forest.

Most noticeable among the Amazon mammals are the monkeys, from howler monkeys to marmosets and tamarins. Jaguars and cougars prowl through the forest grounds or trees, camouflaged by the plants. Sometimes they swim in the river.

The vampire bat, a flying mammal, lives in colonies. A colony usually has less than a hundred bats although a few numbering in the thousands have been reported. The vampire bat feeds on other animals by making a small cut and lapping up blood. The bite doesn't hurt. Many victims sleep through it. The chief problem with vampire bats is in transmitting diseases like rabies.

The Amazon's largest mammals live in the river. The ton-sized manatee, nicknamed a sea cow or water ox, has been hunted for food since colonial times and is endangered. It moves slowly and doesn't see well. Amazonian manatees try to stay away from people and boats. They like the acidic black water, but will move to flooded areas during the wet season. They eat as much as possible during that time because they fast for the dry season.

Many Amazon River dolphins are pink dolphins known as "boto" by Brazilians. They may weigh up to 350 pounds and grow to eight feet. Legend says that these river dolphins are shape shifters who change into handsome men at night. Although there are smaller grey dolphins in the Amazon River, the pink dolphin gathers the most interest, both

Amazon River dolphin

for its size and color. The bubble-gum color is mainly found on males. Some scientists believe the pink is from scar tissue. Male dolphins are very aggressive and fight often. Like many other Amazon animals, they visit the flooded forests, swimming through the trees and snacking on frogs and fish.

River dolphins differ from their ocean cousins. Their longer, skinnier beaks allow them to find food between branches or by digging in the river mud. They can also bend their necks at a 90-degree angle, which helps them when moving through flooded forests. Like all dolphins, the Amazon River dolphin uses echolocation to help find its way. It's estimated that there are about 100,000 Amazon River dolphins left. Some are accidentally killed in fishing nets. Local fishermen also sometimes kill dolphins to use as catfish bait.

Even with all the animal species mentioned, none meets the number of insects. Many live in the trees. "One large tree might have several hundred species of insects associated with it,"[3] says *The Smithsonian Atlas of the Amazon.*

Not all animals are good for the rain forest. Livestock—including cattle, water buffalo, pigs, goats, and sheep—have been introduced to the Amazon. These animals have contributed to the destruction of the rain forest by eating and destroying many plants. Large-scale ranching has also damaged the habitats of many fish species.

The Mystery of Colonel Fawcett

Fawcett

Colonel Percy Harrison Fawcett was a British explorer sent to chart the South American wilderness in 1906 by the Royal Geographic Society in London. Fearless, he thrived in the Amazon jungles. Whereas other people became physically and even mentally ill on expeditions to the Amazon, Fawcett rarely did. In fact, he became very impatient with any weakness in others he traveled with.

He also had little patience for people who would enslave or treat the native people poorly. He had good success meeting and befriending Indian tribes during his travels. One trick that he found quite useful was to play a small flute-like instrument called the recorder or sing to hostile natives. When they calmed down, he gave them gifts as a sign of friendship. Fawcett shared some of the details from his travels with Arthur Conan Doyle, a writer who had become famous by creating the fictional detective Sherlock Holmes. Doyle used Fawcett's information in one of his books, *The Lost World*, about a land of dinosaurs.

Fawcett heard stories and rumors of an ancient city deep within the Amazon. He called the city "Z" and became obsessed with finding it. In 1925, he set off to find it with his oldest son, Jack, and Jack's friend, Raleigh Rimell. None of the men was ever heard from again. Rescuers looked for the men, and some of them were never heard from again either. Even today, the mystery of what happened to Fawcett and whether he ever found the city of Z continues to fascinate people.

Manaus is the largest city on the Amazon River. In addition to a population of nearly two million, Manaus is a port for large ocean liners.

CHAPTER 5

The Amazon River—Today and Tomorrow

Where once only occasional villages could be seen from the Amazon River, today there are large, modern cities set off from the floodplain. The largest city, Manaus, is located close to the middle where the Rio Negro joins the Amazon River. Manaus has almost two million people. Belém, near the mouth of the river, is second with 1.4 million. Boats regularly take travelers to Manaus from Belém in a leisurely trip that takes five to six days. Both of these cities are in Brazil, along with the smaller city of Santarém (population about 275,000), located between the two. Peru's largest city on the Amazon River is Iquitos, with a population of about 400,000.

Over 75 percent of the indigenous people of the Amazon have left for the cities. Those who remain often live in significant poverty with little education or job skills. A typical family income equals the equivalent of about 1,000 U.S. dollars a year.

The Amazon tribes lived without much interference until the last half of the twentieth century, when South American governments decided to colonize the area and built roads and cities. As a result, cultures were destroyed. People whose ancestors had lived by the Amazon River for thousands of years had to assimilate or die.

People who live along the floodplain often have houses on stilts or on higher ground. Still, every few years, the Amazon floods more than normal, and these people must leave their homes. Sometimes temporarily. Sometimes permanently.

More than 350 indigenous tribes or groups have called the Amazon area home. The number of indigenous tribes in the Amazon has dwindled along with the numbers of people in each of the tribes. About 50 tribes have had little or no contact with the outside world. Brazil's government policy is to leave these people alone.

South American economics led to the shrinking of the Amazon rain forest. Ten to 15 percent is already gone. Building cities and towns takes space. So does farming and industries that depend on the river. That means cutting down trees. There is also a demand for lumber from the rain forest trees. Logging is an industry that provides jobs to people.

According to the authors of *Floods of Fortune,* "the Amazon is being transformed by deforestation, urban growth, mining, dams, and widespread exploitation of its natural resources."[1] Deforestation has led to the extinction of many species of life. The rate of deforestation had decreased for awhile. Now, it's on the rise again. The Brazilian Space Research Institute uses satellites to keep track of deforestation of the rain forest. Some scientists predict the entire Amazon rain forest could be gone in two or three centuries.

Destroying the Amazon rain forest creates an imbalance in nature. The Amazon rain forest is the richest ecosystem on Earth. It provides 20 percent of the Earth's oxygen. Climate scientists say that destroying the rain forest puts the Earth at risk by creating more carbon dioxide and increasing global temperatures. Increasing temperatures put biodiversity at risk. "This remarkable biodiversity is one of the reasons

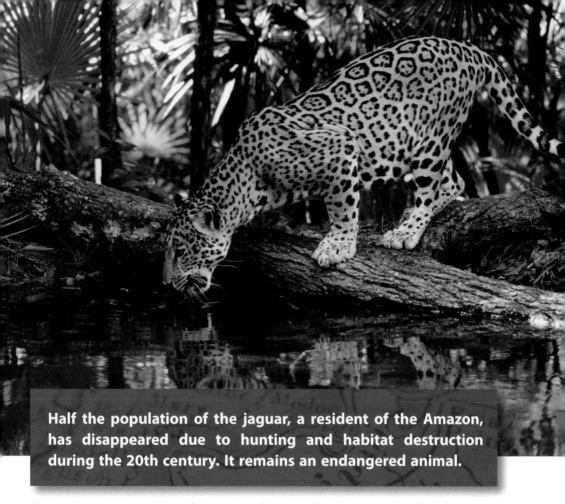

Half the population of the jaguar, a resident of the Amazon, has disappeared due to hunting and habitat destruction during the 20th century. It remains an endangered animal.

that the preservation of the rain forest is so important to all earth's life,"[2] says Richard Lutz.

Currently the chief threat to the Amazon rain forest comes from ranching. Livestock have eaten rain forest plants and trampled on the floating meadows. Hundreds of plants and thousands of invertebrates are gone. Fisheries, necessary for local economies to succeed, are lost without the floating meadows and flooded forests.

The 1980s also saw a gold rush in the Amazon basin. Approximately half a million people found work, but it had unfortunate consequences. Gold mining led to mercury poisoning and the destruction and pollution of streams. Mercury is poisonous to animal and human life.

Swimmer Martin Strel of Slovenia brought attention to the need for clean water by swimming the length of the Amazon River in 2009. According to Strel, "the Amazon is much more mighty"[3] than other rivers.[3]

The Amazon River is also important as a major source of fresh water in a world where fresh water is a concern for the future. The Amazon River and basin have about 20 percent of all the fresh water that flows into the world's oceans. The Amazon River discharges enough water in the Atlantic Ocean each day to meet New York City's water needs for nine years.

There are no bridges crossing the Amazon River. It has no dams either, although some of its tributaries do. Dams are used to create hydroelectric power, an important energy source. Yet damming the river would lead to the extinction of further species of life. Catfish travel from the mouth of the Amazon to spawn in the headwaters in the Andes each year. The pink river dolphins also migrate each year. What would happen to these and other animals if a dam is built on the Amazon River?

The people of Brazil, Peru, and its neighbors are currently arguing about dams in the region. Several dam projects are being planned for places like the Madeira River, Tapajo River, and Araguaia-Tocantins River. All are Amazon tributaries. The most controversial one is the Belo Monte Dam on the Xingu River, a tributary of the Amazon. It would be the world's third largest dam when complete. Opponents say the dam would change the flow of the river. This would destroy a large part of the rain forest. At least ten species of fish would be extinct. Up to 40,000 indigenous people of the Juruna and Arara tribes would be forced from their homes.

The Itaipu Dam was built in the 1980s on the Paraná River between Brazil and Paraguay. People of the Guaraní tribe were forced from their homes. Today, they live in welfare camps on the shores of the Itaipu Reservoir.

The construction of dams is just one of any decisions that will have to be made about the future of the Amazon River. Hopefully, the decisions will benefit everyone.

Big River Men and Guinness World Records

Martin Strel

Martin Strel is a marathon swimmer who hopes his world record swims bring attention to the need for clean water. In 1992, Strel swam the 65 mile (105 kilometers) Krka River in his home country of Slovenia. He did it in 28 hours. When he swam the much longer 1,780-mile (2,865 kilometers) Danube River in 2000, he received the Guinness World Record.

He received his second world record in 2002 for swimming the Mississippi River in 68 days. As Strel conquered the world's rivers, he set his eye on the mighty Amazon.

On February 1, 2007, Strel began his swimming journey in Peru. For 66 days he swam, averaging 50 miles a day. Worried about the piranha, he had an escort boat distract them by pouring blood in the water, away from where he swam. Strel reached the end of the Amazon on April 7. Swimming a distance longer than the width of the Atlantic Ocean, Martin Strel established his third Guinness World Record.

A little over a year later, another environmentalist and adventurer decided to focus on the Amazon River. Ed Stafford from Britain decided to do what no one else had ever done: Walk the length of the Amazon River. He began his journey on April 2, 2008. He finished 860 days later on August 9, 2010. Like Strel, Stafford brought attention to the Amazon River. He also set a Guinness World Record for his achievement.

Chapter Notes

Chapter 1 Cinnamon & Gold
1. Anthony Smith, *Explorers of the Amazon* (New York: Viking, 1990), p. 13.
2. Ibid., p. 73.
3. Ibid., p. 93.

Chapter 2 A River is Born
1. Michael Goulding, Nigel J.H. Smith and Dennis J. Mahar, *Floods of Fortune: Ecology and Economy Along the Amazon* (New York: Columbia Press, 1996), p. 9.
2. Anthony Smith, *Explorers of the Amazon* (New York: Viking, 1990), p. 60.
3. Ohio State University Research, "First Satellite Measurement of Water Volume in Amazon Floodplain." http://researchnews.osu.edu/archive/amflood.htm

Chapter 3 Black, White, and Clear Water
1. Michael Goulding, Nigel J.H. Smith and Dennis J. Mahar, *Floods of Fortune: Ecology and Economy Along the Amazon* (New York: Columbia Press, 1996), p. 5.
2. Ibid., p. 7.
3. Richard L. Lutz, *Hidden Amazon: The Greatest Voyage in Natural History* (Salem, Oregon: DIMI Press, 1999), p. 125.

Even a narrow stretch of the Amazon waters is wide enough for a passenger in a canoe to appreciate.

Chapter 4 Life on the River

1. Michael Goulding, Ronaldo Barthem and Efrem Ferreira, *The Smithsonian Atlas of the Amazon* (Washington, D.C.: Smithsonian Books, 2003), p. 10.
2. Richard L. Lutz, *Hidden Amazon: The Greatest Voyage in Natural History* (Salem, Oregon: DIMI Press, 1999), p. 1.
3. Goulding et. al., *The Smithsonian Atlas of the Amazon*, p. 21.

Chapter 5 The Amazon River--Today and Tomorrow

1. Michael Goulding, Nigel J.H. Smith and Dennis J. Mahar, *Floods of Fortune: Ecology and Economy Along the Amazon*. (New York: Columbia Press, 1996), p. 1.
2. Richard L. Lutz, *Hidden Amazon: The Greatest Voyage in Natural History* (Salem, Oregon: DIMI Press, 1999), p. 1
3. Rachel Cernansky, "Swim the Amazon, Win a Guinness World Record." http://planetgreen.discovery.com/travel-outdoors/swim-amazon-guinness-record. html

Books

Goulding, Michael, and Nigel J.H. Smith and Dennis J. Mahar. *Floods of Fortune: Ecology and Economy Along the Amazon.* New York: Columbia Press, 1996.

Goulding, Michael, and Ronaldo Barthem and Efrem Ferreira. *The Smithsonian Atlas of the Amazon.* Washington: Smithsonian Books, 2003.

Grann, David. *The Lost City Of Z: A Tale of Deadly Obsession In The Amazon.* New York: Doubleday, 2009.

Hemming, John. *Tree of Rivers: The Story of the Amazon.* London: Thames & Hudson, 2008

Lutz, Richard L. *Hidden Amazon: The Greatest Voyage In Natural History.* Salem, Oregon: DIMI Press, 1999.

Smith, Anthony. *Explorers of the Amazon.* New York: Viking, 1990.

Magazines

"The Future of the Forest." *The Economist,* June 13, 2009.
 http://www.economist.com/node/13824446

On the Internet

Amazonia: News
 http://www.amazonia.org.br/english/

Center for Global Environmental Education, Hamline University: Rivers of Life
 http://cgee.hamline.edu/rivers/Resources/river_profiles/Amazon.html

European Commission Research and Innovation: Research Reconstruct Amazon River History
 http://ec.europa.eu/research/headlines/news/article_09_08_05_en.html

International Rivers: Amazon Basin
 http://www.internationalrivers.org/en/node/363?gclid=COyYgOaj6qoCFadgTA od-hDIPQ

PBS: Conquistadors – Orellana – Discovery of Amazonia
 http://www.pbs.org/conquistadors/orellana/orellana_a00.html

Project Amazonas: A Brief History of Amazon Exploration
 http://www.projectamazonas.org/brief-history-amazon-exploration

Science Daily
 Amazon River is 11 Million Years Old
 http://www.sciencedaily.com/releases/2009/07/090707155827.htm
 Amazon River Reversed Flow
 http://www.sciencedaily.com/releases/2006/10/061025085229.htm
 First Satellite Measurement of Water Volume in Amazon Floodplain
 http://www.sciencedaily.com/releases/2010/08/100805172955.htm Books

Books

Aloian, Molly. *The Amazon: River in a Rain Forest.* New York: Crabtree Publishing, 2010.

Berkenkamp, Laurie. *Discover the Amazon: The World's Largest Rain Forest.* White River Junction, Vermont: Nomad Press, 2008.

Heinrichs, Ann. *The Amazon Rain Forest.* Tarrytown, New York: Benchmark Books, 2011.

Montgomery, Sy and Dianne Taylor-Snow. *Encantado: Pink Dolphin of the Amazon.* Boston: Houghton Mifflin Books for Children, 2002.

Woods, Michael. *Seven Natural Wonders of Central and South America.* Minneapolis, Minnesota: Twenty-First Century Books, 2009.

Websites

Discovery Channel
   http://dsc.discovery.com/

Educational Web Adventures: Amazon Interactive
   http://www.eduweb.com/amazon.html

Mongabay: The Amazon: The World's Largest Rain forest
   http://rain forests.mongabay.com/amazon/

National Geographic http: www.nationalgeographic.com
   Rivers
   http://education.nationalgeographic.com/education/encyclopedia/river/
   Few Remaining River Dolphins Indicator of River, Human Health
   http://news.nationalgeographic.com/news/2010/09/photogalleries/
   100907-river-dolphin-pictures/#/freshwater-dolphins-threatened-amazon-
   river_25649_600x450.jpg

Science Kids: Amazon River Facts
   http://www.sciencekids.co.nz/sciencefacts/earth/amazonriver.html

Smithsonian National Zoological Park: Amazonia
   http://nationalzoo.si.edu/animals/amazonia/default.cfm

Glossary

advocate (AD-voh-kate) – to support an idea or plan; also a person who supports such an idea or plan

assimilate (uh-SIM-uh-layt) – to be absorbed into a group or culture

biodiversity (bye-oh-duh-VUHR-suh-tee) – a condition in which a variety of species live in a single area in nature

channel (CHAN-uhl) – a narrow stretch of water between two land areas

circumference (sur-KUHM-fur-uhnss) – the distance around something

conquistador (kon-KEES-ta-dor) – a conqueror and explorer from Spain

current (KUR-uhnt) – the movement of water in a river or ocean

deforestation (dee-FOR-ist-ay-shun) – the process of cutting down forests

economics (ek-uh-NOM-iks) – study of the way money, goods, and services are used in a society

ecosystem (EK-oh-siss-tuhm) – a community of animals and plants interacting with their environment

endangered (en-DAYN-jured) – in danger or at risk of extinction

expedition (ek-spuh-DISH-uhn) – a long journey for a specific purpose

extinction (ek-SINGKT-shun) – complete dying out of an animal or plant

floodplain (FLUHD-playn) – a low area near a stream or river that becomes flooded during heavy rains

friar (FRY-ur) – a man who works for the Roman Catholic church

geology (jee-OHL-uh-jee) – the study of the earth's layers of soil and rock

gorge (GORJ) – a deep valley with steep sides

habitat (HAB-uh-tat) – the place and conditions in which a plant or animal lives

headwaters (HED-waw-terz) – streams that are the source of a river

hydropower (hye-DRO-pow-uhr) – the making of electricity from the force of water

indigenous (in-DIJ-uh-nus) – native to a certain area

invertebrate (in-VUR-tuh-brit) – a creature without a backbone

isotope (EYE-so-tohp) – form of a chemical element with the same physical properties, but different nuclear properties

latex (LAY-teks) – a milky liquid from a plant that makes rubber

marathon (MAR-uh-thon) – a race or competition for a long distance

migrate (MYE-grate) – to move from one region to anther

petroglyph (PE-truh-glif) – a drawing or carving on a rock

plates (PLAYTS) – one of the sheets of rock that compose the earth's outer crust

pod (PAHD) – a long case that holds the seeds of certain plants

sediment (SED-uh-muhnt) – small rocks, sand, or dirt carried by water or wind

silt (SILT) – fine particles of matter carried by flowing water

tributaries (TRIB-yuh-ter-ees) – streams or rivers that flow into a larger stream or river

uranium (yu-RAY-nee-uhm) – a chemical element that is radioactive

watershed (WAW-tur-shed) – the land area that drains into a river or lake

Index

Acuña, Cristobal de (Father)   8

Amapá   18

Amazon Basin   16-18, 24, 26, 27, 39, 40

Amazon rainforest   17, 22, 24, 26, 28, 33, 34, 38-40

Amazons (warriors)   8, 11

Andes Mountains   6, 10, 15, 19- 21, 24, 25, 28, 40

Arequipa   19

Atlantic Ocean   8, 15, 18, 25, 30, 40, 41

Bolivia   21, 25

Brazil   8, 16, 18, 19, 21, 22, 25, 33, 36, 38, 40

Colombia   15, 21

Danube River   41

Doyle, Arthur Conan   35

Ecuador   4, 15, 21

El Dorado   6

Fawcett, Jack   35

Fawcett, Percy Harrison (Colonel)   30, 35

French Guiana   9

Godin, Isabel   9, 10

Godin, Jean   9

Goodrich, B.F.   27

Guinness World Record   41

Incas   4

Iquitos   36

Krka River   41

Lost World, The   35

Manaus   25-27, 35, 36

Maraňon River   15

Mississippi River   16, 41

Nevado Mismi   19, 25

New York City   40

Nile River   12, 15, 19

Orellana, Francisco de   4, 7, 8, 10, 11, 25

Pangaea   12

Peru   16, 19, 21, 25, 36, 40, 41

Pinzón, Vicente Yánez   8

Pizarro, Francisco   4, 6

Pizarro, Gonzalo   4, 6-8

Quito   4, 8, 9

Rio Negro   22, 25, 36

Royal Geographic Society   35

Sherlock Holmes   36

Tapajós River   22

Teixeira, Pedro   8, 10

Tocantins-Araguaia Rivers   22

Trombetas River   22

Ucayali River   15, 19

Venezuela   21, 25

Wonder Woman   11

Xingu River   22, 27, 40

zircon   12

ABOUT THE AUTHOR

Karen Bush Gibson is the author of more than 30 educational books about various places, cultures, historical events, and people. She is very interested in the environment and loves to travel to new, exciting places.